EXTRAORDIN SEA CREATURES

Contents

A Watery World

Beneath Earth's oceans are secret worlds packed with living things. Millions of beautiful and bizarre animals make their homes here, from creatures too small to see to the largest animals living on Earth — the blue whales.

Ocean Earth

More than two-thirds of the earth is covered in seawater. This huge mass of water is divided into four main areas, called oceans. The Pacific Ocean is the biggest, the Atlantic and Indian oceans follow, and the Arctic Ocean is the smallest. The oceans are then divided into smaller areas called seas.

Arctic Ocean

N

North America

Europe

Asia

Atlantic Ocean

Pacific Ocean

South America

Africa

Indian Ocean

Pacific Ocean

Australia

Antarctica

Exploring the Deep

How do we know what lies beneath the ocean? Well, scientists dive down to explore, collecting information about the animals and plants that they find. Scientists use underwater cameras to take photos, too. But there's still a whole lot that we don't know.

EXTRA! EXTRA!
Scientists think that clown fish use the sea anemones to protect them from enemies. In return, clown fish may clean the anemones and drive away anemone-eating fish!

Clown fish swim among purple sea anemones — animals that look like plants. The anemone's stinging tentacles are harmless to the clown fish because the fish's body is protected by slime!

Coral Reef

This scene looks like an underwater yard full of tiny trees and flowers — but this is a coral reef. Many sea creatures make their homes among the coral, including sea horses and brightly colored fish. Surprisingly, corals are animals, not plants!

Coral Pals

A single coral is called a polyp. Most polyps are the size of one of your fingernails. The polyps cluster together in groups called colonies, to form clumps of coral. There are hundreds of different kinds of coral, and their colonies come in all shapes and sizes.

"Let's stick together!"

▲ Coral builds up into a large, brittle, chalky mass, known as a reef.

That's Weird!

Among coral's worst enemies is the crown-of-thorns sea star. This sea star eats by pushing its stomach out of its body to cover a piece of coral. Then it dissolves the coral and sucks it into its belly. Slurp!

Clam Clamper

The giant clam has a soft body and lives inside a hard shell among the coral. If in danger, it slowly clamps the two parts of its massive shell shut. At 4 feet (1.2 m) long, the shell is so huge that you could take a bath in it.

Dad Is Mom

Now you can be the mom!

Sea horses are just one of the strange creatures that live on coral reefs. You might not guess it, but sea horses are fish! Their looks aren't the only odd thing about them, though. They also have an unusual way of having babies. The female lays her eggs in a pouch on the male's belly, and he looks after them until they hatch.

Sharks Galore!

Lean, mean, eating machines — sharks live in all the oceans and are fierce hunters. Most sharks have streamlined, torpedo-shaped bodies that glide well through the water, making them fast swimmers.

  This basking shark may be a big mouth, but luckily it doesn't attack people! It eats by gulping down seawater and straining out tiny sea animals, called plankton.

The Eyes Have It

Hammerheads are named for their weird heads. There's an eye at each end of the hammer, which probably helps them sense their prey, or victims, better.

Neat Nibbler

One kind of shark sinks its teeth into its victim's skin, then takes out a cookie-shaped bite. You may have guessed its name — the cookiecutter shark! It's also known as the cigar shark.

Cookies, anyone?

That's Weird!

The wobbegong shark prefers the low life on the ocean floor to the high life near the water's surface. With its flattened body and patchy skin, this shark looks a lot like a piece of old carpet. Don't try wiping your feet on it, though. The wobbegong has a short fuse and can easily turn nasty!

What makes sharks so scary?

No false teeth for me!

Hunting sharks have hundreds of jagged-edged teeth. The teeth grow in rows, so if one breaks or falls out, a tooth from the row behind moves forward to take its place.

Dinner's ready!

A shark is excellent at homing in on its next meal. It can sense tiny amounts of blood in the water from a wounded animal far away. Then it speeds in for the kill.

Are you my dinner?

Yikes!

A few kinds of shark attack people! Usually, a shark only bites you if it mistakes you for its usual prey. Every year, fewer than 100 people are attacked.

Dolphin Fun!

Scientists believe that dolphins are one of the most intelligent animals in the world. They may even have the same brain power as humans! Dolphins are also sociable animals and they live together in groups, called schools.

TRUE STORY!

There are lots of cases around the world where lone dolphins make friendly contact with people. However, in Monkey Mia, Australia, groups of dolphins have been coming to the shore to greet visitors since the 1960s. People are not allowed to feed the dolphins because, although they are friendly, they are still wild animals.

It's great to meet you!

Sing-along

Dolphins travel and hunt in a group, and communicate with one another by sound. They make high-pitched noises that sound like clicks, whistles, and squeaks. Sometimes, dolphins even sound as though they're singing!

Bottle-nosed dolphins play together, leaping out of the water at the same time. No one knows why dolphins leap and somersault. They may be signaling to other dolphins, or just having fun.

"Sing along with us!"

Family Circle

Although dolphins live in the water, they are mammals, not fish. This means that, like humans, they breathe air and their babies feed on their mother's milk. They live in big families, so when a dolphin mother gives birth, there's often an aunt ready to help her, like a nurse.

Beware: Poison!

One way to scare enemies is to pack a painful punch — with poison! Many sea creatures are venomous, which means that they bite, sting, or inject poison in other ways.

Deadly Jelly

The box jellyfish can be as big as a football, with as many as 60 stinging tentacles hanging down from its body. Each tentacle is up to 15 feet (4.5 m) long — nearly as long as a giraffe is tall! Its sting is so painful that this jellyfish is nicknamed the sea wasp. Thousands of people are stung by sea wasps every year, but thanks to a drug developed in the 1970s, most of them recover.

Wow!

The blue-ringed octopus isn't much bigger than your hand. But its beak can give you a sharp bite and its tiny body has enough poison to paralyze 10 adults. Luckily, it's shy and rarely comes close to people.

Go away, I'm shy!

Killer Snake!

There are 50 different kinds of sea snakes and they are all venomous. Fortunately, most of them prefer to stay out of the way. The deadliest is the olive sea snake, which is even more deadly than the most venomous land snake. So watch out!

I'm REALLY dangerous!

Eek!

Stone Dead

The most venomous fish in the world is called the stonefish. It gets its name because it hangs out on the seabed, posing as a rock. It's hard to see and its poisonous spines are piercingly sharp, ready to dig in deep!

Fooled you!

EXTRA! EXTRA!
Watch out! The lionfish will sting you if you are in its way. But don't worry too much — its poison rarely kills people.

Q. WHAT LIES ON THE SEABED AND QUIVERS?   A. A NERVOUS WRECK!

This lionfish may look like a bathing beauty, but its fringes hide poison-packed spines. It uses its fins to steer small fish and trap them against the coral reef. Then it strikes!

Hide-and-Seek

Many sea creatures spend their time cruising for a meal. One way of hiding from these hungry attackers is to use camouflage — smart disguises that help animals blend into the surroundings.

EXTRA! EXTRA!
The pygmy sea horse is the world's smallest sea horse. It grows to only 0.8 inch (2 cm) — about half the length of your thumb!

It is nearly impossible for divers to spot the tiny pygmy sea horse. Its body patterns and coloring almost exactly match the coral in which it lives.

Spot That Fish

Butterfly fish live on coral reefs, where their bright stripes help them hide against the background of brightly colored corals. This fish has an eyelike dark spot on its back, so that enemies can't tell its head from its tail and don't know which end to attack!

Clever Cuttlefish

1 The cuttlefish is a master of disguise. To hide, it changes its skin color to match different surroundings.

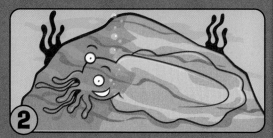

2 One minute it's sandy like a rock. The next, it's as gray as the seabed or as greenish-brown as seaweed.

3 But if its quick-change act doesn't work, the cuttlefish can still escape. It covers its tracks by squirting a cloud of brown ink at its enemy!

Eyes can see you!

Sandy Secret

Sharks and other big sea creatures like to eat flatfish, such as flounder and sole. Flatfish hide by burying themselves in the seabed. To keep sand out of their eyes, they have an unusual eye arrangement. Most fish have an eye on each side of their head, but flatfish have both eyes on one side — the top side!

That's Weird!

The decorator crab collects underwater junk to hide itself. It attaches anything it can find to its sticky shell — from seaweed and sand to living sea anemones and coral polyps.

Crusty Creatures

Crustaceans, such as crabs, lobsters, and shrimp, are boneless animals whose soft bodies and jointed legs are covered and protected by a tough, outer shell. There are more than 40,000 different types of these crusty creatures on Earth and most of them live underwater.

Getting Crabby

Don't fiddle around with this male fiddler crab. One of its two claws is huge. The crab uses it to wave hello to females. But make a fiddler crab mad, and this claw will give you a nasty pinch.

Wow!

Crabs might seem like creaky, awkward creatures, but don't be fooled. The ghost crab can run faster than you can walk — at an amazing 4 miles per hour (6.5 kph)!

Hey, want to race?

Ready, Aim, Fire!

Most lobsters and some shrimp have claws, too. The pistol shrimp has a big claw, which it uses in a clever way. It snaps the claw shut to make a noise like a pistol firing. Stunned by the noise, its prey is unable to defend itself from attack. This is how the pistol shrimp got its name.

CRACK!

EXTRA! EXTRA!
As the hermit crab grows, its home becomes a tight squeeze. When this happens, it moves to a new home!

HA HA

Unlike most crustaceans, the hermit crab doesn't have its own shell. It usually lives in the empty shell of a sea snail, or finds shelter in holes in bits of wood, rock, or coral.

Feeding Time!

Under the sea, it's eat or be eaten! When dinnertime arrives, many strange things begin to happen underneath the waves. Every animal needs to watch out, or it could be on someone else's dinner menu.

Shock Tactics

The Atlantic torpedo ray's table manners are simply shocking. It generates its own electricity so it can knock out other fish and eat them without a struggle. One shock from a big torpedo ray is enough to stun a fully grown person — or power a microwave!

Jelly Belly

1 Here, fishy fishy...

The Portuguese man-of-war looks like a single jellyfish, but it's actually made up of hundreds of tiny creatures. Some of these creatures form tentacles that kill fish. Others then do the actual eating!

2 YIKES!

But the man-of-war has enemies! The blue sea slug nibbles its tentacles and even steals its poison. It does this by eating the poison cells and storing them in its body to defend itself from attackers.

Open Wide!

It's not hard to guess that the gulper eel has a huge appetite. This eel is a deep-sea fish with a body that's nearly all stomach and mouth. The gulper eel can open its jaws wide enough to gobble down creatures that are as big as itself — gulp!

Sea slugs eat other small sea creatures, such as coral. Most sea slugs do this by scraping off bits of food with a large, rough tongue called a radula, which works like a nail file.

That's Weird!

The hagfish is a slimy, eellike fish. It's blind, so it uses feelers around its mouth to find its favorite snack: dead or dying fish. It protects itself by producing a load of slime to cover its skin. Enemies simply slide off it!

YUCK!

Muddy Munchies

One of the messiest underwater eaters is the gray whale. This ocean giant grubs for its grub in the seabed, sucking up mouthfuls of water and mud, and straining out shrimp and other tasty tidbits.

Smart Octopus!

If you're looking for an underwater brainiac, then here's the creature for you! The octopus knows all sorts of clever ways to stay alive. It can even figure out how to remove a cork and take food from inside a bottle!

All Head and Legs

There are more than 100 different kinds of octopus. They all have a soft, boneless headlike body with eight trailing tentacles attached to it. An octopus uses its tentacles to pull itself across the ocean floor, on the hunt for tasty crabs, clams, and snails.

Wow!

If an enemy approaches, the octopus has a cool way to escape. It can squeeze its rubbery body through the tiniest of holes in the rock. In fact, all an octopus needs for an escape route is a hole the size of one of its eyes.

Disappearing Act

When the octopus needs to escape an enemy, first it changes color to blend in with its background. If the enemy comes too close, the octopus turns white with fear. It pumps out an inky black cloud to hide its getaway, then jets off backward. It does this by sucking water into its body and pumping it out again — whoosh!

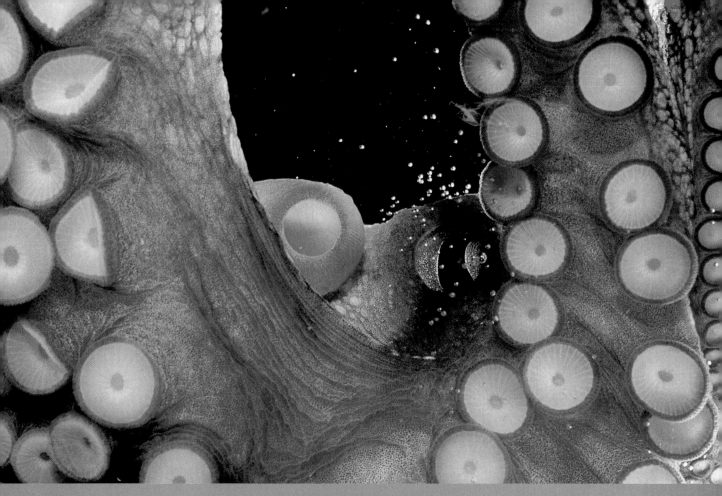

Don't arm wrestle an octopus! Each of its tentacles is lined with suckers, which stick to its prey and are almost impossible to unstick. One type of octopus has about 2,000 suckers!

Copycat Creature

1 The mimic octopus is a real smarty-pants. When it wants to hide, it changes its shape and color to copy other creatures.

2 To escape from the poisonous sea snake, the mimic octopus just copies it! It flattens its body and stretches out its arms.

3 In fact, the mimic octopus is so clever that it can copy a flatfish. But why it would want to do that, nobody knows!

Underwater Forests

Kelp is giant seaweed that can grow as high as a 20-story building, up to 200 feet (60 m). Swimming around in the sunlit kelp is like gliding through a green, leafy underwater forest.

EXTRA! EXTRA!
Giant kelp can shoot up 18 inches (46 cm) a day. If you grew that quickly, you'd be as tall as a house in two weeks!

Kelp needs sunlight to grow. Like most other seaweeds, it fixes itself by an anchorlike part, called a holdfast, to rocks or the seabed near the coast.

Cuddly Cuties

The sea otter makes its home in the kelp. It spends nearly all its life in the water, floating on its back. It even eats lying down, using its belly as a table. It snacks on everything from clams and sea urchins to crabs, fish, and squid. When it sleeps, it wraps itself in kelp so that it doesn't drift away.

Tight Squeeze

The swell shark is a camouflage king. It is covered with dark brown patches that make it hard to spot among the kelp and the rocks on the seabed. But if it is spotted by an enemy, it has an unusual escape tactic. It slides into a crack in the rocks. Then it wedges itself in by filling its belly with water and swelling up like a balloon. It fits in the crack so tightly that a predator, or attacker, can't pull it out!

Who

lives among the kelp?

Chomp, chomp

The sea urchin is a small, round, spiny creature. Sometimes, it nibbles on the kelp, just like an underwater lawnmower, and even destroys huge areas of it!

Can you see me?

A giant kelpfish can be a range of colors, from brown to silver, to camouflage it among the waving leaves of the kelp. Enemies find it hard to spot!

Delicious!

A sea star is a star-shaped creature, which hides around the base of the kelp. It feeds on rotting trash on the soft, muddy seabed. Yum!

Out in the Cold!

How would you like to live in a refrigerator? In the polar regions, the extreme north and south of the world, creatures such as killer whales, seals, and seabirds cope with water that rarely goes above freezing — brrrr!

Sea Singer

When the beluga whale is hunting, its whitish yellow skin helps it to hide among the ice in the Arctic Ocean. All whales make songlike noises, but the beluga is such a loud singer that it's been nicknamed the sea canary.

Wow!

Billions of pinkish, shrimplike creatures called krill live in the cold seas. In summer there can be so many that the water turns pink. Krill are the favorite food of huge animals, like the blue whale, which can eat 30 million krill in a day. That's three big truckloads!

Yum, here's my dinner!

HA HA

EXTRA! EXTRA!

Killer whales love to leap, and may be seen leaping with other killer whales. They live in groups, called pods, which contain up to 50 members.

The killer whale, or orca, belongs to the dolphin family. It lives in all the oceans, but especially in cold regions.

How

do polar animals beat the freeze?

Sea mammals, such as whales, have a layer of thick fat, or blubber, under their skin to keep them warm. It's a little like wearing an extra sweater!

Penguins stay warm and cozy, too. As well as blubber, a penguin has soft, downy feathers that work like a thick quilt.

I'm as warm as toast!

The Antarctic icefish has a clever way of beating the cold. There are chemicals in its blood that keep its body from freezing.

Sea Monster!

If you think monsters really exist, then you're right! Under the oceans live lots of giant-sized creatures. But although they look like big bullies, most of them are pretty harmless.

EXTRA! EXTRA!
Manta rays are related to sharks. Their triangular-shaped bodies gave them the name *manta*, which means "cloak" in Spanish!

Is it a fish or a plane? This manta ray flies through the water on wide, winglike fins. It's almost as big as a hang glider — as much as 22 feet (6.7 m) from fin tip to fin tip!

Fantastic Fish

The world's largest fish is the whale shark. In spite of its enormous, gaping mouth there's no need to be scared. The whale shark is just a big, shy softie — it mostly eats krill. At 40 feet (12 m) long, there's enough room for three family cars to park on its back!

Record Breaker

Big sea creatures look like tiny babies in comparison with the enormous blue whale. This sea mammal grows to more than 90 feet (27 m) long — as long as two basketball courts. It's the biggest of all living creatures.

Wow!

The blue whale gives birth to a supersize baby with an enormous appetite! It sucks down as much of its mother's milk in one day as a dairy cow produces in a whole year!

Burp!

Eyes Wide Open!

The Atlantic giant squid has the biggest eye of any living animal. At 20 inches (50 cm) across, it's 20 times bigger than one of yours!

BOO!

HA HA

Deep Down Under

The deeper you go in the ocean, the darker and colder it becomes. Fewer creatures are able to survive here. There are some very odd creatures, with strange ways of staying alive.

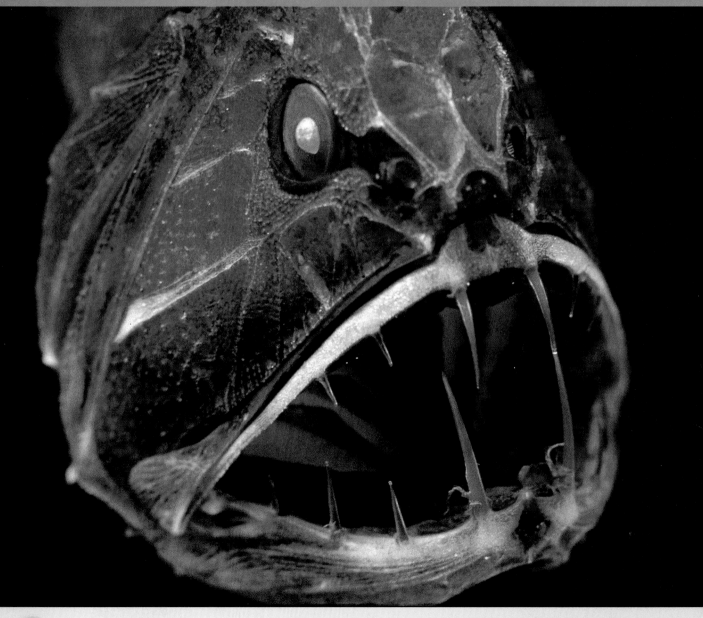

 There's not much food at the bottom of the ocean, so the fangtooth fish eats just about anything! It opens its mouth and swallows fish and crustaceans that fall from above.

What's the Big Attraction?

The anglerfish is a bright spark when it comes to lighting up the dark ocean depths. An extra-long fin with a glowing tip sticks out from the top of its head. This attracts other fish to it like moths to a candle. Fish swim straight into its gaping mouth.

Give It a Rest

Fins come in handy when you're a deep-sea fish. When the tripod fish is tired, it rests on its tail and two extra-long fins. That's how it got its name — a tripod is a three-legged stand or stool. While the tripod fish rests, its fins stop it from sinking into the muddy ocean floor. At the same time, it can wait for a tasty snack to swim by.

Fishy Flasher

The lantern fish's belly looks as though a row of party lights is strung along it. Although the lantern fish often attracts prey with these body lights, the lights also help it hide from enemies. Its glowing belly matches the sunlight or moonlight shining on the sea's surface, and makes it invisible to big fish swimming below.

That's Weird!

There's no escape if you're scared of spiders, even deep down on the ocean floor. Sea spiders have 10 or 12 legs, but they are still related to eight-legged land spiders. Sea spiders feed on soft-bodied deep-sea creatures by sucking the liquid from their bodies. Yuck!

Extra Amazing

Amazed by sea creatures? Want to know even more about the secrets of the deep? Dive into these wild and wacky, watery facts!

Cracking Crabs

The sandy seabed off the coast of Japan is home to the world's biggest crustacean, the giant spider crab. The body of this king-sized crab isn't much larger than a football, but its outstretched legs can span 9 feet (3 m). Here, inside a tank, a diver comes close to one of them.

Marine Midget

The smallest fish in the world is also the world's smallest animal with a backbone — at less than 0.35 inch (1 cm) long, it could fit on one of your fingernails. The tiny fish is called the dwarf goby and it lives in the Indian Ocean.

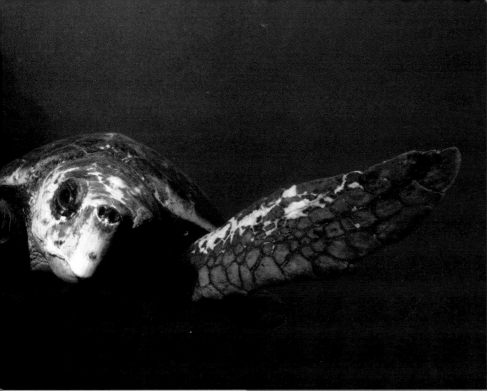

Wandering Ways

The loggerhead turtle is well traveled! It nests and lays its eggs on beaches in warm parts of the world. After nesting, it swims thousands of miles to areas rich in food. It then returns, usually to exactly the same site, to nest again. Every year, it may swim up to 6,000 miles (10,000 km).

Fastest Fish

The fastest thing on fins is the sailfish. This speedy creature has been clocked at an amazing 68 miles per hour (109 kmh), which is a fraction faster than the land-speed record holder, the cheetah.

I can beat you!

Super Starfish

Imagine a sea star that's bigger than your bathtub! The disk-shaped middle of the world's largest sea star is about the same size as a bath plug. From arm tip to arm tip, though, it measures well over 4 feet (1.2 m). Sea stars are related to sea urchins.

Hi, there!

The Living Dead

Scientists used to think the ancient fish called the coelacanth died out 80 million years ago. Then, in 1938, fishermen made a strange catch off the coast of South Africa. The fish was so bizarre that they sent it to a museum to be identified. Sure enough, it was a coelacanth, so who knows what else is out there!

True or False?

Are you an ocean expert? Test your knowledge and say whether you think these statements are true or false. Answers are on page 32, but no cheating!

1. The Atlantic is the biggest ocean.

2. Baby sea horses hatch from their father's pouch, not their mother's.

3. Hundreds of people are killed by sharks every year.

4. This creature is known as the sawhead shark.

5. The stonefish is the world's most venomous fish.

6. Dolphins are very intelligent.

Ocean Terms

Antarctica
The huge ice-covered area of land that covers and surrounds the South Pole. Antarctica is the world's iciest and coldest place.

Arctic
The cold region that surrounds and covers the North Pole. The Arctic isn't one block of land. Instead it is mainly frozen ocean, plus Greenland and the northernmost parts of Canada, Russia, Alaska, and Iceland.

blubber
The thick layer of fat beneath the skin of sea creatures such as whales and seals. This helps to keep their bodies warm.

camouflage
How an animal is colored or patterned to blend in with its background and make it hard to see.

coral
A tiny sea animal, related to sea anemones. The soft body of a coral is surrounded and protected by a chalky, cup-shaped skeleton.

crustacean
Crabs, lobsters, and shrimp belong to this animal group. Instead of a skeleton inside their body, most crustaceans have a tough outside shell.

7. The sea wasp is an insect.

8. The olive sea snake is the most venomous snake on Earth.

9. Hermit crabs grow their own shells.

10. Shrimp are related to crabs.

11. The pistol shrimp fires bullets to kill its prey.

12. This animal is the world's largest fish.

13. An octopus's body is protected by a tough outside shell.

14. Octopuses turn white with fright.

15. Seaweed can grow as tall as trees.

16. This creature uses its stomach as a dinner table.

17. Whales sound like they sing.

18. The blue whale has the world's largest eye.

19. There are no spiders in the ocean.

20. The cookiecutter shark eats cookies.

fin
One of a fish's paddlelike body parts. Fish use their fins to push themselves through the water, as well as to help them balance and steer in different directions.

fish
A legless animal that has a backbone and lives in water. Fish don't breathe air. Instead, they take oxygen from the water through body parts called gills.

mammal
An animal with a backbone that breathes air, and whose young feed on milk made in the mother's body. Most mammals live on land, but some live in the sea, including whales and dolphins.

plankton
Tiny animals and plants that drift in seas and lakes near the water's surface. Most of them can only be seen through a microscope.

predator
An animal that hunts and kills other animals for food.

prey
An animal that is hunted and killed for food.

tentacle
Slim, bendy body parts, which grow from the head of animals such as octopuses and sea anemones. These animals use their tentacles like arms and hands — to feel things, and to catch food and carry it to their mouths.

Index

Answers

1 False	11 False
2 True	12 False
3 False	13 False
4 False	14 True
5 True	15 True
6 True	16 True
7 False	17 True
8 True	18 False
9 False	19 False
10 True	20 False

Author: Jackie Gaff
Illustrations: Andy Hamilton
Consultant: Dr. Margaret Rostron
Photographs: Cover: Coral Grouper, Red Sea, Pictor; p. 2 Corbis/Stephen Frink; p. 3 Powerstock/Zefa; pp. 4–5 OSF/Mark Webster; p. 6 BBC Natural History Unit/Alan James; p. 7 Corbis/Jeffrey L. Rotman; pp. 8–9 OSF/Konrad Wothe; p. 10 FLPA/Panda/K. Atkin; p. 11 Pictor; p. 12 NHPA/B. Jones and M. Shimlock; p. 13 Bruce Coleman/Pacific Stock; p. 14 OSF/David B. Fleetham; p. 15 FLPA/ Dembinsky/Susan Blanchet; p. 17 Ardea/Kurt Amsler; p. 18 Bruce Coleman/ Pacific Stock; p. 19 NHPA/ Daniel Heuclin; p. 20 BBC Natural History Unit/Jeff Rotman; p. 21 FLPA/Minden Pictures/F. Lanting; pp. 22–23 Bruce Coleman/ Pacific Stock; p. 24 Bruce Coleman/Jim Watt; p. 25 Ardea/ Ron and Val Taylor; p. 26 NHPA/Norbert Wu; p. 27 NHPA/Agence Nature; p. 28 left Jeffrey L. Rotman; pp. 28–29 Corbis/Stephen Frink.

Created by act-two for Scholastic Inc. Copyright © act-two, 2001
All rights reserved. Published by Scholastic Inc.

SCHOLASTIC and associated logos are trademarks and/or registered trademarks of Scholastic Inc.

No part of this publication may be reproduced in whole or in part, or stored in a retrieval system, or transmitted in any form or by any means, electronic, mechanical, photocopying, recording, or otherwise, without written permission of the publisher. For information regarding permission, write to Scholastic Inc., Attention: Permissions Department, 555 Broadway, New York, NY 10012.

ISBN 0-439-28604-2

12 11 10 9 8 7 6 5 4   3 4 5 6/0

Printed in the U.S.A.

First Scholastic printing, November 2001